1. Aberdeen
2. Aberdeenshire
3. Arran & Ayrshire
4. Northern Argyll
5. Southern Argyll
6. The Borders
7. The Cairngorms
8. Caithness & Sutherland
9. Dumfries and Galloway
10. Dundee & Angus
11. Edinburgh
12. Fife, Kinross & Clackmannan
13. Glasgow
14. Inverness
17. Lochaber
18. Loch Lomond, Cowal & Bute
19. The Lothians
20. Moray
21. Orkney
22. The Outer Hebrides
23. Perthshire
24. Ross & Cromarty
25. Royal Deeside
26. Shetland
27. Stirling & The Trossachs

The remaining two books, Distinguished Distilleries and Scotland's Mountains, feature locations throughout the country so are not included in the above list.

PICTURING SCOTLAND

PERTHSHIRE

2 Perhaps the ultimate evocation of the fairy-tale fortress: magnificent Blair Castle stands in splendour amidst a scenic symphony that creates a perfect view. See also pages 101–104.

PERTHSHIRE

Welcome to Perthshire!

Perthshire is a county of contrasts and records: the world's tallest hedge (opposite), the smallest distillery, the sole survivor from Shakespeare's 'Birnam Wood' and the oldest living thing in Europe, if not the planet! From the city of Perth with its population of approximately 43,000 to highland villages like Kinloch Rannoch, it embraces communities of all sizes. A largely rural county, its landscape includes rich farmland growing everything from grain to soft fruit and, at the other end of the spectrum, some of Scotland's wildest country. Ben Lawers, Scotland's tenth highest peak, towers over the expanse of Loch Tay, while the northern parts of the county are home to some of the country's most inaccessible Munros (Scottish mountains over 3,000ft/914m). Whatever your taste in scenery, it will be found somewhere in this characterful county.

Perthshire has witnessed more than its share of Scotland's history-in-the-making, with kings enthroned on Moot Hill, former location of the Stone of Scone, just north of Perth. Going back to earlier times, the Picts told their stories through carvings on standing stones, some of which have survived to provide the county with perhaps its most fascinating relics. Some of the most important of these are featured. Many of Scotland's most famous – and notorious – personalities have made their name or left their mark here: the bard Ossian; Macbeth; William Wallace; Robert

Left: Meikleour beech hedge, 30 metres/100 ft high and 530 metres/third-of-a-mile long stretches along the A93 south of Blairgowrie. Right: 1885 drinking fountain, The Square, Aberfeldy.

the Bruce; Mary, Queen of Scots; Rob Roy MacGregor; Bonnie Prince Charlie; Sir Walter Scott. Some say that Pontius Pilate was born in the village of Fortingall, Glen Lyon (see p.70).

This book aims to convey something of that variety by means of a photographic tour around the county. Starting in the city of Perth itself, we then investigate its environs before setting off to explore further afield. We shall cross the county a number of times, starting by working from east to west across its southern districts, then heading north for a while before crossing back from west to east through the central area. From the eastern side there will be another step north, before a final east-to-west transit through the mountains and along the lochs to the north-west corner of Perthshire.

It should be said that, like all other counties, Perthshire's boundaries have changed over the years. In recent times it has lost its south-western part to Stirling District, but we shall dip into this area in acknowledgement of its recent past. Conversely, Perthshire absorbed the former county of Kinross to the south; however, we shall not venture there as this area falls more naturally into another region of Scotland that will be the subject of another book in this series. Therefore, this book defines Perthshire in terms of present-day administrative boundaries rather than historic ones, with the exception of Kinross for the reason noted above.

The city of Perth can trace its roots back to the 10th century, a settlement being established there about 150 years before it became a royal burgh around 1125. It was a natural place for a settlement, at the lowest fording (later, bridging) point of Scotland's longest and most volatile river, the Tay. The aerial picture opposite gives a good idea of the city's layout, looking south. The numbers refer to the page in this book on which that building/feature is illustrated.

Perth from the air, looking south. The numbers mark the location of places illustrated in this book – see last paragraph opposite.

8 From Perth Bridge, looking north along the Tay with North Inch Park on the far side of the river.

10 An interesting contrast in shapes reaching to the sky: a modern sculpture in the Norrie-Miller Park on the east bank of the Tay, and across the river St Matthew's Church.

The same park exhibits a number of such sculptures, which reward investigation of their thought-provoking shapes.

12 Perth Bridge, built in 1766 by John Smeaton and widened in 1869 by A.D. Stewart. The Tay has demolished a number of earlier bridges on or near this site.

A view from Perth Bridge looking south along Tay Street.
The buildings show off a fine array of finials and other forms of ornamentation.

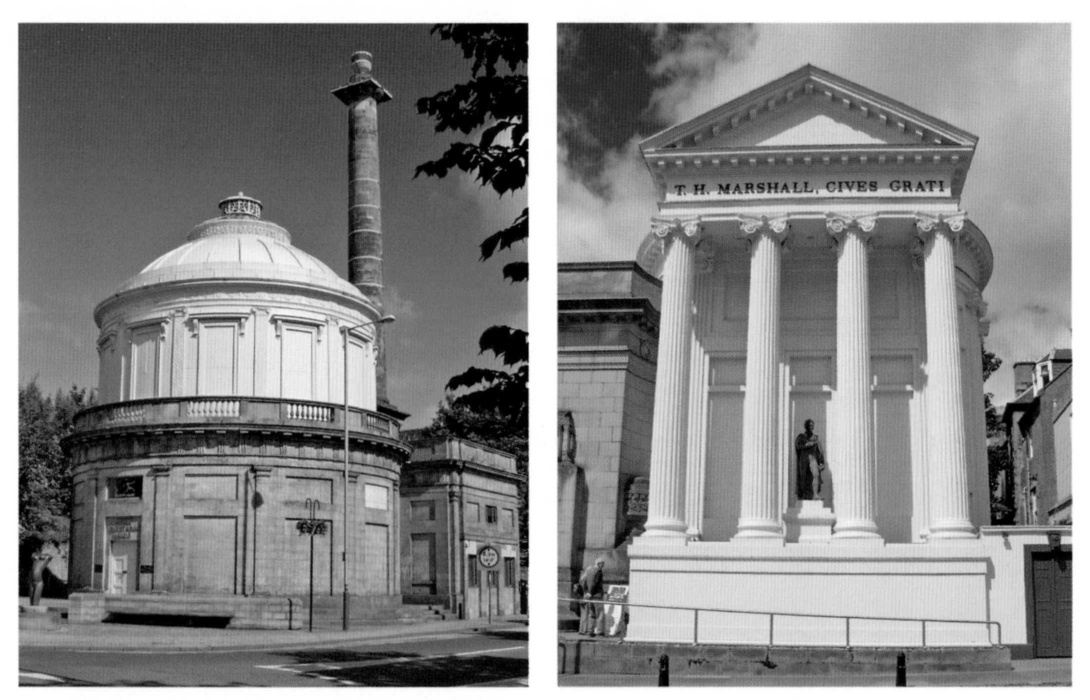

14 Left: The old water-pumping station built in 1822 is now the Fergusson Gallery, home to the largest collection of work by the Scottish artist, John Duncan Fergusson. Right: Perth Museum & Art Gallery.

Fine and Applied Art displayed at Perth Museum and Art Gallery, one of the oldest museums in the UK with more than half-a-million objects in its Recognised Collection of National Significance.

16 St John's Kirk is the oldest standing building in Perth and one of the most important parish churches in Scotland. The original building was completed in 1241 and the leaded spire in place by 1511.

The interior of St John's. The best-known incident to take place here was John Knox's sermon against idolatry preached in 1559. The church underwent a major restoration in 1923. Inset: roof boss.

18 St John's Street, to the east of the Kirk, demonstrates fine architecture and a variety of sculptures attached to the lamp posts.

Perth's former City Hall. At the time of writing, its future is uncertain, with demolition a distinct possibility, so let's enjoy it while we can. Note the statues at top left and top right of the building.

20 Known as the Fair Maid's House, on North Port, this ancient dwelling is so named because of its fanciful connection to the heroine of *The Fair Maid of Perth* by Sir Walter Scott (1771-1832).

Left: the 18th-century Hal o' the Wynd House, West Mill St., also features in the novel *The Fair Maid of Perth*. Right: This memorial in the North Inch pays tribute to the 51st Highland Division.

22 This impressive new metal sculpture of a group of thistles (Scotland's national flower) stands at the Charlotte Street entrance to North Inch Park.

The Lower City Mills which today house Perth's Tourist Information Centre were once grain mills using water power from a lade (channel – see inset) dug from a tributary of the Tay.

24 Perth Concert Hall is Scotland's newest concert hall: it opened in 2005. Built as a millennium project, it has a dazzling glass-fronted foyer and copper-topped dome hall with a stunning auditorium and

elegant studio. Before building work began, an archaeological dig was carried out. The dig uncovered evidence of a medieval castle, first documented in the 12th century but destroyed by flood in 1209.

26 Perth city centre is book-ended by its two great parks, the North Inch that we have already seen and the South Inch, seen here. This avenue of trees lines Marshall Place.

This view across South Inch frames the church of St Leonard's-in-the-Fields. The construction of this fine building goes back to 1883.

28 A classic view of Perth and the River Tay, looking north from Queen's Bridge. Flood defences completed in 2001 give the city much better protection from the river than in former times.

Continuing across Queen's Bridge brings us to Rodney Gardens, where the statue *Evergreen* by Kenny Munro is made from granite and bronze and represents the many spires of the churches in Perth.

30 Floral detail in Branklyn Garden, which contains over 3,000 plant species in just under 1.75 acres. Now a National Trust for Scotland property, it was created by John and Dorothy Renton.

In the foreground is Perth harbour and Moncrieffe Island. Beyond, eastern Perthshire stretches away along the Tay estuary almost to Dundee. On the left is the famous viewpoint of Kinnoull Hill.

32 And from Kinnoull Hill: the folly on the left was built in the 19th century. Further on, a patch of sunlight shows up the countryside colours around Kinfauns Castle (a private estate).

The dramatic cliffs and steep wooded slopes of Kinnoull Hill are now seen from Elcho Castle (see p.37) with the River Tay and some rich farmland in the foreground.

34 Scone Palace, just north of Perth. In 1803 the 3rd Earl of Mansfield employed William Atkinson to rebuild the medieval house into a gothic palace with echoes of the monastic original.

The Drawing Room at Scone. Its Regency opulence is accentuated by treasures from Versailles, most notably the writing desk seen at bottom left of the picture, presented by Marie Antoinette.

36 Stanley Mills, a few miles north of Scone, began textile manufacturing in 1787 and were in production until 1989. Recently restored, they are open to the public as a Historic Scotland site.

Just east of Perth on the south side of the Tay stands Elcho Castle, a remarkably complete 16th-century fortified mansion. Open to visitors under the auspices of Historic Scotland.

38 Continuing into eastern Perthshire but now north of the Tay, this is the recently restored 18th-century Cumberland Barracks in the market town of Coupar Angus.

Some of the 26 Pictish carved stones on display at Meigle Sculptured Stone Museum. They make up one of the most important collections of early medieval sculpture in Western Europe.

40 Eastern Perthshire contains much of the county's best farm land. Here in Strathmore, the combine harvester takes a break from gathering the grain under a lovely September sky.

CLAAS

42 A couple of miles north of Meigle is the small town of Alyth, attractively set around the Alyth Burn. An ancient settlement, it is recorded as being in existence by the 11th century.

Now moving just west of Perth, Huntingtower Castle comprises two fine and complete tower houses. Also known as The House of Ruthven, it is another excellent Historic Scotland location.

44 Left: south-west of Perth is the village of Dunning which is graced by St Serf's Church.
Right: it houses the Dupplin Cross, a masterpiece of Pictish stonework.

Continuing south-west from Dunning we reach the town of Auchterarder, nicknamed the ‘Lang Toun’ thanks to its mile-and-a-half long High Street, at the western end of which is this pleasant park.

46 Running south from Auchterarder into the Ochil Hills, the famous Glen Eagles is seen in full winter garb.

The world-famous Gleneagles golf courses have been providing one of the finest settings for the sport for 90 years. The Gleneagles Hotel opened in 1924.

48 A real rarity: Tullibardine Chapel is one of the most complete and unaltered medieval churches in Scotland, founded in 1446. It is located two miles north-west of Auchterarder.

Continuing north-west we come to the pleasant village of Muthill and the interesting ruins of another important medieval church. The Romanesque tower is similar to that of Dunning church.

50 Innerpeffray Library near Muthill is the oldest free public lending library in Scotland, founded in 1680. The present building dates to 1762 and contains about 5,000 books.

Striking northwards now, this westerly view from the hills above Gilmerton (near Crieff) captures the essence and variety of Perthshire: agriculture, forest, glens and mountains.

52 A few miles further north is the Sma' Glen, a famously beautiful stretch of Glen Almond. The blend of textures, form and colours combine to create a perfect scene.

Returning south to the outskirts of Crieff, Glenturret is the oldest malt whisky distillery. Established in 1775, it is the home of the *Famous Grouse* and offers distillery tours and tastings.

54 Crieff is the main town of Strathearn, with a population of almost 6,000 and lying on the southern edge of the Scottish Highlands. This is James Square that marks the town centre.

Crieff has been a holiday resort since Victorian times and is the second-largest town in Perthshire. The turrets of the famous Crieff Hydro can be seen on the skyline of this picture.

56 Drummond Castle, between Muthill and Crieff, was built around 1490 and its gardens initially laid out in the early 17th century by John Drummond, 2nd Earl of Perth. After the Second World War,

with a reduced workforce, the decision was taken to simplify the gardens. However, with their ancient yew hedges and copper beeches, they remain some of the finest formal gardens in Scotland.

58 The attractive village of Comrie is west of Crieff on the River Earn and the Highland Boundary Fault. The hilltop monument commemorates Henry Dundas, first Lord Melville.

Dalginross Bridge and 'The White Church'. Built in 1805, the church is Comrie's most distinctive landmark. Grade A listed, in 1965 it became the village community centre.

60 A few miles further west, St Fillans is exquisitely situated at the eastern end of Loch Earn. The village takes its name from St Fillan, an Irish monk who came to Scotland in 717.

A different impression of Loch Earn, seen here from its southern shore and stretching into the mountainous distance. The loch is approximately 10.5kms/6.5 miles long.

62 From former Perthshire territory west of Loch Earn, we now look east down steep Glen Ogle to mighty Ben Vorlich, 985m/3232ft. The old railway track-bed can just be seen, bottom right.

Perthshire also used to include the town of Callander, above which Ben Ledi (879m/2885ft) provides a perfect place for viewing Ben Lawers (1214m/3983ft), about 20 miles away to the north.

64 The delightful village of Killin at the head of Loch Tay also now belongs to Stirling District, but many residents still feel allied to Perthshire. The Falls of Dochart cascade through the village.

Having seen a distant view of Ben Lawers, it's now time for a closer inspection. Its peak is seen here from Beinn Ghlas (1103m/3619ft), another Munro which is traversed en route to Ben Lawers.

66 From the summit of Ben Lawers, a birds-eye view down into Glen Lyon, which lies to the north of the Lawers range.

North-east from Ben Lawers are two more Munros, An Stuc on the left and Meall Garbh to its right (both 1118m/3668ft). These three mountains surround Lochan nan Cat.

68 At the eastern end of Loch Tay is the Scottish Crannog Centre, where an example of this Iron Age type of loch dwelling has been re-constructed to enable visitors a taste of this life.

Perthshire has many stone circles and standing stones. The most complete example is Croft Moraig, about two miles east of Loch Tay. It is a complex double circle that dates back over 5,000 years.

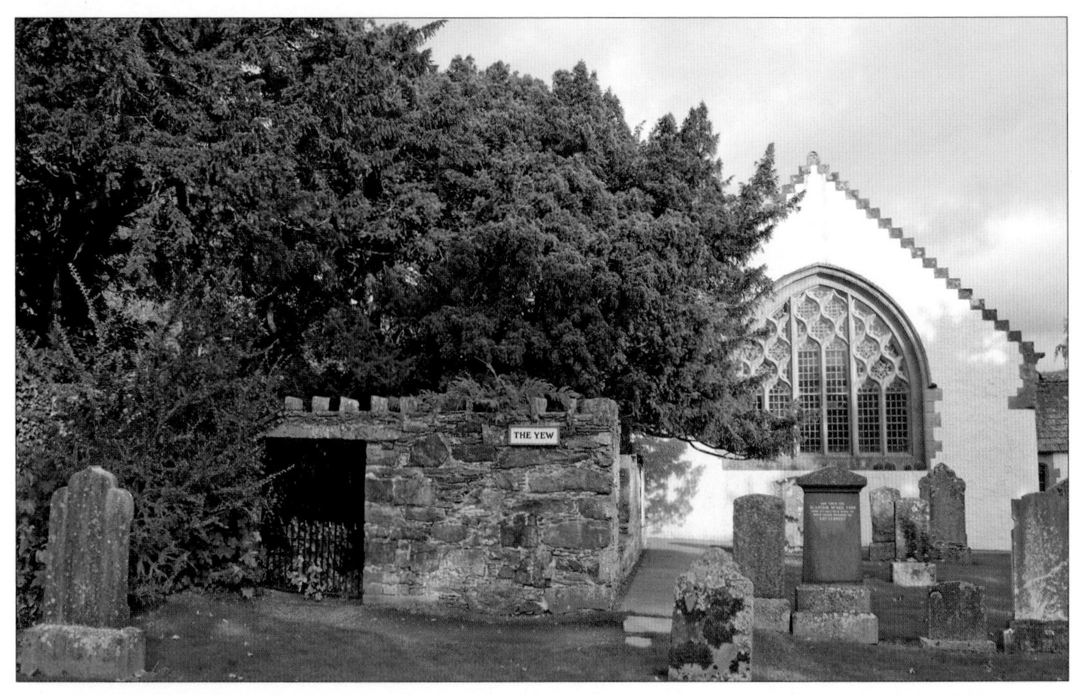

70 Fortingall village in Glen Lyon is where to find this ancient Yew tree: Europe's – and possibly the world's – oldest living thing. Scholars believe its roots go back as much as 5,000 years.

Glen Lyon lies to the north of Loch Tay and is lined by mountains. Left: Creag Mhor (981m/3218ft) stands imposingly above Fortingall. Right: Glen Lyon from the gorge west of Fortingall.

72 From the hillside above the eastern end of Loch Tay, the village of Kenmore looks appealing in its surrounding gown of autumn colours. Kenmore as seen today was built by the Earl of Breadalbane

as a planned estate village in the 1750s. The Kenmore Hotel lays claim to being the oldest inn in Scotland. Kenmore is an excellent base from which to explore the county.

74 A change of mood now as we return to Glen Lyon to see it in winter, looking towards the gorge seen in the right-hand picture on p.71.

Visitors to Perthshire are spoiled for choice when it comes to scenic glens. This is Glen Lyon in early autumn, looking down the glen from just east of Bridge of Balgie.

76 Journeying east down Strath Tay brings us to Castle Menzies, seat of Clan Menzies for over 400 years. Prince Charles Edward Stuart's death mask can be seen here.

It's just a short distance on to Aberfeldy, entered via Lt. General Wade's bridge, opened to traffic at the end of October 1733. Almost 400ft in overall length, the centre arch measures 60ft.

78 Aberfeldy has much to see and, especially in autumn, the Birks of Aberfeldy are high on the list. The Moness Burn tumbles down a gorge into the town offering cameos like this and . . .

. . . broader canvases like the scene above. Originally known as the Den of Moness, the area was renamed after a song written by Robert Burns following his visit in August 1787.

80 On the edge of Aberfeldy, Dewar's World of Whisky offers an interactive exhibition that educates and entertains. The experience includes a guided distillery tour and whisky tasting.

A few miles east of Aberfeldy, the River Tay at Grandtully is the main base for canoe and kayak slalom activities and racing in Scotland. Here, a youngster learns how t manage the rapids.

82 The historic town of Dunkeld has much to see including the Ell Shop (left), named after the weaver's measure on the wall outside. Inset: Ell shop detail referring to the National Trust for Scotland.

Dunkeld was proclaimed the first ecclesiastical capital of Scotland by Scotland's first king, Kenneth MacAlpin. The majestic ruin of the cathedral still dominates Dunkeld today (see also back cover).

84 Across the Tay from Dunkeld is the Hermitage, home of some of Britain's tallest trees and the Black Linn Falls, pictured here from Ossian's Hall. Wordsworth, Mendelssohn and Turner have all walked here.

Adjoining Dunkeld to the south is the village of Birnam. Beatrix Potter enjoyed family visits here and her influence has left its mark in the form of these familiar characters in the Beatrix Potter Garden.

86 From Dunkeld, an easterly meander through the hills brings us to the textile town of Blairgowrie where the River Ericht provided a ready source of water power.

Today Blairgowrie has a more diverse economy. This is the Wellmeadow which, complete with the War Memorial, forms an attractive centrepiece to the town.

88 Heading north from Blairgowrie and onto the Strath Ardle road at Bridge of Cally leads to a scene which captures the upland essence of Perthshire. On this road that goes over to Pitlochry and looking

back into upper Strath Ardle above the village of Straloch, the enticing patchwork of heathery slopes, rocky outcrops and forestry plantations demand our attention.

90 Going the other way at Bridge of Cally takes us up famous Glen Shee. In this view south of Spittal of Glenshee, a landscape sequence culminates in the mountains around Glas Tulaichean.

From Spittal of Glenshee, the Cairnwell (933m/3061ft) stands on the border with Aberdeenshire amid the Cairngorm mountains. Evidence of skiing paraphernalia can be seen on the summit.

92 The Loch of the Lowes near Dunkeld is a wildlife reserve with a visitor centre run by the Scottish Wildlife Trust. Many bird species including ospreys can be seen, as well as red squirrels.

An idyllic setting for Edradour Distillery, Scotland's smallest. It is situated just off the route from Strath Ardle (pp.88-89) which brings us westwards over the hills to Pitlochry.

94 And in Pitlochry, the historic Blair Athol Distillery also welcomes visitors and treats them to a sample of the produce. That aside, the distilleries have much charm and architectural interest.

Pitlochry is spectacularly set amid the Perthshire hills, with Ben Vrackie (840m/2755ft) forming a splendid backdrop and offering a tempting hill walk.

96 Beautiful Loch Faskally sits beside Pitlochry. The hydro-power dam which created the loch has a salmon ladder alongside it, giving visitors the chance to see these fish in action.

The story behind Pitlochry's Festival Theatre can be traced back to the vision arising from John Stewart's visit to the town in 1944. Today's theatre building was opened in 1981.

98 Killiecrankie Pass, north of Pitlochry, echoed to the sound of battle in July 1689. Redcoat soldier Donald McBane escaped by making a spectacular leap across the river at this point.

A little way downstream from Killiecrankie, the River Garry widens out and shows its gentle side, making it a lovely place to enjoy.

100 For many, Queen's View (referring to Queen Isabella, wife of Robert the Bruce), Loch Tummel, presents the perfect blend of Scottish scenery. The mountain on the left is Schiehallion, 1083m/3553ft.

Moving a few miles north, this angle on Blair Castle is not the classic one (see pp.2-3) but gives a good idea of its extent and complexity. The earliest known part of the present castle dates from 1269.

This is the magnificent drawing room which represents the pinnacle of the 2nd Duke's aspirations to grandeur. Visitors can enjoy a tour of the castle interior.

Blair Castle is the HQ of Europe's last remaining private army, the Atholl Highlanders. They are seen here parading at the annual Atholl Gathering, which takes place on the Bank Holiday weekend . . .

104 . . . at the end of May. There is so much to enjoy and do at Blair Castle that many visitors return again and again, always discovering something new. These deer live in the castle's deer park.

The estate village of Blair Atholl: low evening sun highlights the lines of the sturdy but stylish buildings. The village is also home to the Atholl Country Life Museum.

106 Blair Atholl station. This train connects London and other English cities directly with Perthshire on its way to Inverness and is an excellent way of travelling to the region.

Just north of Blair Atholl, behind the House of Bruar, are the Falls of Bruar. Left: water erosion has created a natural stone arch at the lower falls. Right: the upper falls justify the 2.5kms/1.5 mile walk.

108 The last leg of the journey takes us westwards from Blair Atholl up Strath Tummel, eventually to reach Loch Rannoch and the village of Kinloch Rannoch in remote north-western Perthshire.

From the summit of Craig Varr, a closer look at the village. The front cover picture of this book was also taken from here, looking the other way over Dunalastair Water to Schiehallion.

110 From near the eastern end of Loch Rannoch, late afternoon light on the view back towards Kinloch Rannoch.

And finally, a long-range shot from Craig Varr. The distant mountains are 30 miles away in Glen Coe, Lochaber – but that's another story and another tour . . .

Published 2012 by Ness Publishing, 47 Academy Street, Elgin, Moray, IV30 1LR. Reprinted 2014.
Phone/fax 01343 549663 www.nesspublishing.co.uk
(First edition published in 2008 entitled Perthshire: a pictorial souvenir).

ISBN 978-1-906549-33-6

Front cover: Dunalastair Water and Schiehallion; p.1: cottage in Fortingall; p.4: metal-sculpted porter at Pitlochry station; this page: a lively burn on Rannoch Moor; back cover: 1809 bridge, Dunkeld

For a list of websites and phone numbers please turn over >

Websites and phone numbers (where available) for principal places featured in this book in order of appearance:

Perthshire: www.perthshire.co.uk (T) 0845 225 5121
Perth: www.perthcity.co.uk
Perthshire Visitor Centre: www.macbeth.co.uk (T) 01738 787696
Meikleour Beech Hedge and Fortingall Yew: www.perthshirebigtreecountry.co.uk
Fergusson Gallery & Perth Museum and Gallery: www.pkc.gov.uk/museums (T) 01738 783425
St John's Kirk, Perth: www.st-johns-kirk.co.uk
Perth Concert Hall: www.horsecross.co.uk (T) 01738 621031
Branklyn Garden: www.nts.org.uk
Kinnoull Hill: www.walkingstories.com
Scone Palace: www.scone-palace.co.uk (T) 01738 552300
Stanley Mills: www.historic-scotland.gov.uk (T) 01738 828268
Elcho Castle: www.historic-scotland.gov.uk (T) 01738 639998
Coupar Angus: www.coupar-angus.org
Meigle Sculptured Stone Museum: www.historic-scotland.gov.uk (T) 01828 640612
Huntingtower Castle: www.historic-scotland.gov.uk (T) 01738 627231
Dupplin Cross: www.historic-scotland.gov.uk
Auchterarder: www.auchterarder.org
Gleneagles: www.gleneagles.com (T) 0800 389 3737
Tullibardine Chapel: www.historic-scotland.gov.uk
Muthill Old Church: www.historic-scotland.gov.uk
Innerpeffray Library: www.innerpeffraylibrary.co.uk (T) 01764 652819
Glenturret Distillery: www.edringtongroup.com (T) 01764 656565
Drummond Castle Gardens: www.drummondcastlegardens.co.uk (T) 01764 681433
Comrie: www.comrie.org.uk
Ben Lawers: www.nts.org.uk (T) 01567 820988